THE CONDOM BOOK
FOR GIRLS

An OPTIMA book
© Alison Everitt, 1990

First published in 1990 by
Macdonald Optima, a division of
Macdonald & Co. (Publishers) Ltd

A member of Maxwell Macmillan Pergamon Publishing Corporation

British Library Cataloguing in Publication Data
Everitt, Alison
    The condom book for girls.
    I. Title
    828.91409

ISBN 0 356 19605 4

Macdonald & Co. (Publishers) Ltd
Orbit House
1 New Fetter Lane
London EC4A 1AR

Typeset in Century Schoolbook by
Leaper & Gard Ltd, Bristol, England

Printed and bound in Great Britain by
The Guernsey Press Co. Ltd, Guernsey, Channel Islands

THE CONDOM BOOK
FOR GIRLS

This book is dedicated to anyone who has ever used a condom . . .
. . . or SHOULD have!

is a freelance cartoonist, writer and frequenter of cafés.

Her work has featured in many women's magazines, but this is the first time she has been let loose on the general public with a book.

en don't like using condoms, it's a well-known fact. They'll use every excuse under the sun, like, "But I'm *allergic* to rubber" … "Aren't you supposed to *swallow* them?" … and, of course, the classic, "Don't worry, I'll be *careful*" … in the vain hope that you've had your BRAIN removed and will believe them!

No-one is terribly keen on using any form of contraception, but it's vital if you want to avoid having a house full of kids, and these days if you want to mingle your private parts with more than one man in your lifetime, condoms are better for your health than anything else. (Except not doing it at all.)

Being pretty ignorant of Grown-Up bodily functions, I used to be rather in the dark about what those things I'd see lying around on pavements on rainy days were used for. When the girls at school would giggle and snort and say they were for . . . you know . . . *DOING IT* . . . I didn't believe them.

I couldn't see how you could practise making babies with something that was all limp and wrinkly.

— I had a lot to learn, eh girls?? . . .

The Conception of
the Condom

omeone must have dreamed them up. I mean, we may have seen them lying around when out for woodland walks with Grandma, but Nature didn't put them there. Well, it DID . . . in a way . . . if you get my drift.

We can safely presume a man invented them, because women haven't been able to do much until recently. (But you can guarantee it was a WOMAN who got him to do it!)

It would have been better if a woman HAD invented them ... who else could envisage a man in nothing but a smile and a piece of pink rubber who *still* thought he was SEXY!

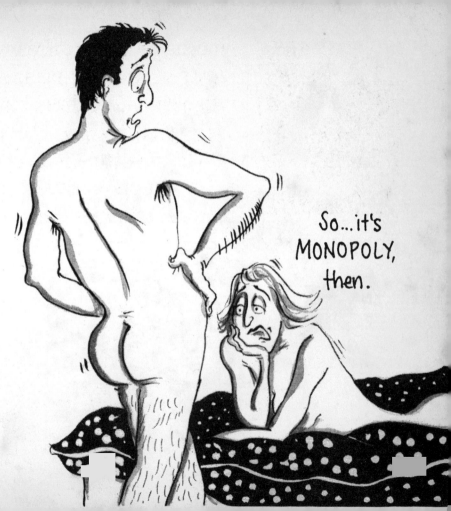

THE CONDOM THROUGH HISTORY

The Romans were tops in the road-building department, but judging by the rate at which their Empire spread, they weren't too hot at contraception . . .

... I blame too many orgies and not enough sex education at school ...

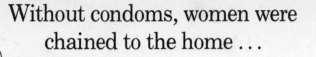

Henry VIII was renowned for nipping off for romps in the hay. Elizabeth I couldn't risk a ruined reputation, so she sent explorers off to find effective methods of contraception, so she could have a good time without bringing *heirs* into it ...

...I doubt whether she had expected the potato!

Before the condom as we know it was designed, it was made of cat gut, pig's bladder or fish membrane. (*LOVELY!*) This kind was generally inefficient, and often WASHABLE!

It is said that Casanova was a great user of this kind of condom. Boy, he must have been some *SMOOTH TALKER!*

Before the Swingin' Sixties were the Frustrated Fifties, where holding hands and getting hot under the collar was as far as you went. (Or so you told your parents . . .)

... Unfortunately, this meant that women faced snatched moments of passion in uncomfortable places, unwanted pregnancies, and the development of the "Three-Minute-Wonder!"

By the Seventies, men had perfected all their EXCUSES ...
It'll be, like, NATURAL LOVE, man...

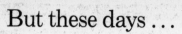

But these days ...

Condom Shopping

ou can get them all over the place these days. Years ago you could only buy them from barber shops, chemists and the odd men's lav. Now all self-respecting shops sell them, and even GIRLS are allowed to carry them about. At least now people can buy them without being embarrassed ...

Can I have some...
...er... co...
cough mixture?
...For me MUM.
...You needn't be embarrassed these days.
...There you go...
CONDOMS

There's no need to be SHY, love...
...If you WANT condoms, ...just ASK!
...ER...no... I...er...
CHEMIST
CONDOMS
THWACK!

Now there are more places to go to buy condoms, you can pick and choose. So ... do you travel out of town to avoid local shops knowing all your BUSINESS? ...

Hello, luv! More JOHNNIES, is it?

URGENT! MAIL ORDER CONDOMS!

... Can you trust the post to arrive on time? (And what if there are malicious PARCEL-STABBERS at the sorting office?)

... or would you be completely blasé about the whole thing, and buy six-monthly packs from Boots?

In an ideal world, we would talk about condoms without Grannies thinking we're BRAZEN, carry them about without men thinking we're EASY, and ask Mum what to do with them without her passing out!

Here you are, dear...
... use them WELL...

... But those days are a long way off, so we have to find effective ways of HIDING them.

Condom Concealment

o matter how old you are, whether you're a teenager or a forty-year-old divorcee-of-three: if your parents find you in possession of a condom, you're in TROUBLE!! ...

(... one way or another ...)

Your parents want you to settle down with a "*nice young man*" ... but they don't want you to PRACTISE until you FIND one.

So, if you want them to think that you're still their little girl, you not only have to hide your condoms, but you also have to learn to do it PROPERLY! ...

When putting them in your pockets,
BEWARE! Parents are not stupid.
DON'T wear flimsy clothes, as they
will stand out like a sore thumb.
(Or a packet of condoms.)

DON'T wear a winter
overcoat in the middle
of a heatwave, just
because the pockets
are bigger ...

... and remember ... some people make a LIVING from the contents of other people's pockets. You may find yourself filling out embarrassing forms at your local nick.

Avoid transparent bags.
... Unless you're
completely brazen or
touting for business.

The size of your
bag depends on
how many
condoms you
decide to take with
you ...

... we're quite subtle,
and only take a few, to
cover accidents, etc ...

The fashion world even accommodates condoms. Men have condom-pockets in their UNDERPANTS. (I wonder why.)

... But WE need them in as many places as we can GET!

VOILÀ! RATS!

BEWARE the man
with a six-pack.
This doesn't necessarily
mean he has a large
sexual capacity ...
more like it takes him
that long to get it
RIGHT!!

Application and Disposal

en seem to assume that girls know from birth how to put on a condom. There's even that handy little paragraph on the back of the packet which says we can put it on for him as "part of love-making".
WHO ARE THEY KIDDING?

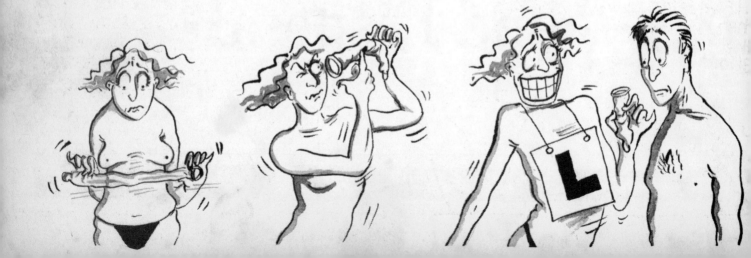

But you can tell a lot about a man by his reaction to our efforts ...

So ... you thought you'd **FLUSH IT DOWN THE LOO?**

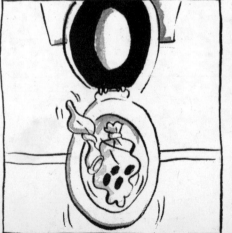

GIBBER
GIBBER

A novel idea would be if someone invented a courier service direct to childless couples . . . cheaper than a Sperm Bank!

Blunders in Benidorm

O holiday, where passion flows as freely as sangria (and is as available) you always have to take and use condoms . . . particularly if you're attracted to foreign parts.

. . . You don't know WHERE those foreign parts have been . . .

The first thing you have to do is to work out where to put them so they don't show up on the airport X-ray machines. You could try stuffing them in your spare pair of knickers, but the BEST way to make sure you go through quickly is to put them in some TAMPON BOXES ...

Strange things happen to holidaying British women. At home they'll pack their suitcases with condoms, full of good intentions ...
BUT ...

(MISS PRISSY KNICKERS)

... as soon as they hit a hot climate, all sense flies straight out of the window, and they turn into sex-mad vamps whose condoms never leave their travel bags ...

The RADAR comes out as soon as they land, and they won't be off the coach five minutes before they've fixed up dates with at least twenty Spanish men, and have declared undying love to half of them ...

¿Cuàl es CONDON?

They're smooth, shifty, and you can trust them as far as you can spit a rat: but it's not surprising we go running at the drop of a sombrero when you take a look at OUR LOT ...

You'd think it would sink in that fifty weeks of lager-swilling has radically affected the state of their bodies, and it really is going to look HORRIBLE when they strip off!

...You'd also think they'd diet and concentrate on getting a tan, but, oh no ... they spend their time drinking, dancing and sucking love-bites so they never have the TIME to sit in the sun.

But obviously some women think this is attractive, because they not only SNOG these chaps, but they exchange BODY FLUIDS as well! They also act as if they had an invisible protective shield around them, so they can mingle with as many men as they like, and not CATCH anything ...

... But they could find themselves taking home more than a few sombreros and their quota of DUTY-FREES ...

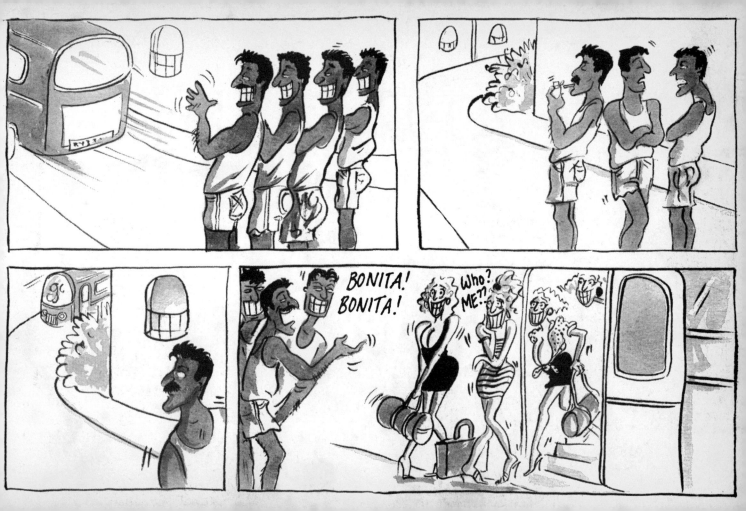

Men and Condoms

he first thing a man does on contact with a condom is to blow it up or fill it with water.

They're very keen to *buy* condoms, *fiddle* with condoms and *wave* them under your nose. The only thing they AREN'T keen to do with condoms is USE THEM!

Mine's **BIGGER** than this, girls!

This sort of activity is meant to IMPRESS US. What they don't realise is that it doesn't help them when they want to fill it with something ELSE later on . . .

It looked better with the GOLDFISH in it...

Chaps have such a HARD time during PUBERTY. They have to cope with problems like …

…working out the EXACT capacity a condom can hold …

…perfecting their "OUTSIDE 50" technique …

…but most of all, the changes to their metabolism. This begins with their EYES …

... they begin to see us as if we were feathered. Hence we become known as BIRDS, and we're treated with as much respect as anyone can a creature whose main function in life is to breed, build nests and plop on people's heads.

...Remember, men will say ANYTHING to get you to Do The Deed ... *AND* to get out of using condoms ...

... and we BELIEVE them: but only when we're ... ... completely naïve ...

... completely smitten ...

...or completely STUPID!

There's a strong link between men, alcohol, and condoms. WE have to consume a lot to hide their faults . . .

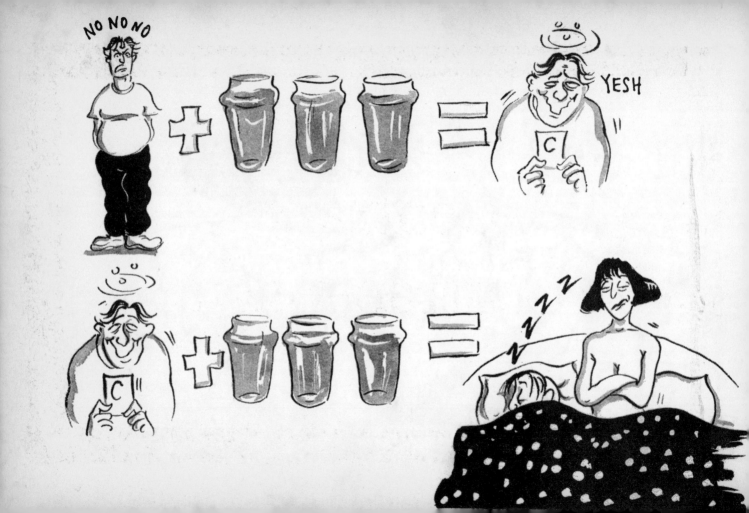

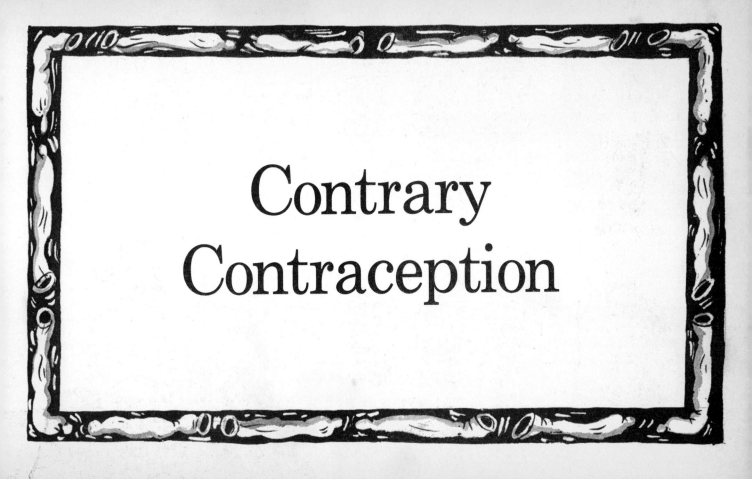

Contrary
Contraception

lthough we are mainly concerned with the ups and downs of the male condom, we can't neglect the fact that there are many other forms of contraception. The condom is, of course, the ONLY form that men actually use ... and they STILL moan about it! ...

...But I used one LAST time!

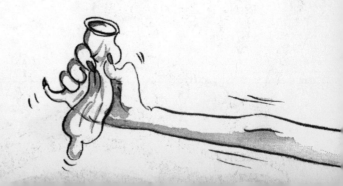

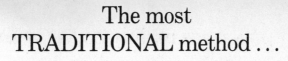

THE PILL

This is fine if you don't suffer from side-effects and are in a monogamous relationship, as you can enjoy spontaneous rubber-free fun without fear of infection.

(Obviously there are women who don't like the idea of chemicals swilling inside them. I say, rather that than TRIPLETS!)

Downers

As well as NOT being "safe sex", you also have to have an EXTREMELY good memory . . .

THE MORNING-AFTER PILL

This is used as a last resort, when MISTAKES are made. It involves getting to your doctor as quickly as possible.

You're not on the PILL??

Downers Apart from having to face a doctor first thing in the morning, it might make you feel rather queasy, which will put you RIGHT off the opposite sex for a LONG TIME!

Have a PRACTICE.

THE CAP

This is a popular form of contraception, as it gives women the power to decide when it's the right time to pop it in.

Downers As well as not being "safe sex", you find that you *can't* "just pop it in". It's an ALMIGHTY PAIN to do! There's no paragraph here to tell MEN to do it "as part of love-making". More often it's a case of trial and error … but mostly ERROR!

THE COIL

This has to be professionally inserted, and stays inside you for years. It is, however, NOT for the squeamish. If you don't like it when your nose is blocked up, you're hardly likely to enjoy having your UTERUS plugged!

Downers

You could be used as a spare TV ariel.

THE FEMALE CONDOM

THE SPONGE

Downers

These two forms of contraception are still in their infancy. Perhaps we should wait until more results are known before trying for ourselves. Unless, of course, you fancy being a GUINEA PIG ...

THE RHYTHM METHOD

If you're not very good at those "*If it takes a man blah blah hours to do blah blah blah*" sums, then you don't stand much chance at this. As far as *I'm* concerned, the only 'safe' period is when you're fast asleep, and *HE*'s on the bus home!

WITHDRAWAL

You MUST remember, whether you're fourteen or forty: no matter WHAT a man says to you in a steamy embrace when you find yourself without any condoms, DO NOT BELIEVE HIM! Trusting him to take it out at the last minute is ALMOST as stupid as letting him put it there in the FIRST PLACE!

Downers

If you don't want to end up with a sudden interest in Mothercare dungarees, or trips to clinics specialising in dodgy wedding-tackle, remember this ... you can trust the last four methods as much as you can trust the GAS MAN arriving when he said he would!

To Conclude

here are all sorts of condoms around at the moment. Every type suits a different purpose, and you can change them to suit your moods. There are ribbed ones, coloured ones, flavoured ones, hypo-allergenic ones, featherlite, super-strong, luminous and *musical* ones, and extra-strong, super-dooper ones for chaps who like to do it with chaps. Unfortunately, they aren't yet bio-degradable, so the GREENEST condom would be an EDIBLE one ...

... any takers??

For every condom, there's
a man to suit it . . .

The
Cave-Man

The
Macho-Man

Super
Thriller

Spotted
DICK

No
Hoper.

DISADVANTAGES OF THE CONDOM

... It's SMELLY:
You may end up thinking
you're living with
Michelin Man!

... It's FIDDLY:
Nothing that a bit of
effort and genuine
lust can't fix.

ADVANTAGES OF THE CONDOM

If you mingle with the toilet parts of a new man, or a total stranger, it is a relief if you used a condom. This helps you to avoid the "BIG 'O'" …

The "Kitemark" ensures that each condom has been electronically tested for performance and reliability. Pity there's not something similar for *men*!

Wear your
condom with
PRIDE !!

All Optima books are available at your bookshop or news-agent, or can be ordered from the following address:

Optima, Cash Sales Department,
PO Box 11, Falmouth, Cornwall TR10 9EN

Please send cheque or postal order (no currency), and allow 60p for postage and packing for the first book, plus 25p for the second book and 15p for each additional book ordered up to a maximum charge of £1.90 in the UK.

Customers in Eire and BFPO please allow 60p for the first book, 25p for the second book plus 15p per copy for the next 7 books, thereafter 9p per book.

Overseas customers please allow £1.25 for postage and packing for the first book and 28p per copy for each additional book.